KT-509-164

BOROUGH

OF

GUILDFORD

PUBLIC

LIBRARY

SERVICE

ISSUE PERIOD ~~TANT~~ DAYS. ~~FINES 6d. per~~
WEEK OR PART OF A WEEK.

REGULATIONS

1. The Guildford Library Service is available to all who live, work or go to school in the Borough of Guildford.
2. Intending borrowers not resident in the Borough of Guildford may have full use of the library service provided that their application for membership is sanctioned.
3. Temporary visitors to the Borough will be admitted as users of the library on production of their home library ticket.
4. Each intending borrower, unless he is a temporary visitor, must fill in an application card and present it, together with an address check, to the librarian at the central library or any branch library.
5. Borrowers under 18 must be recommended by a parent, guardian, or employer who should sign the application card.
6. Each borrower may have one ordinary ticket, on which one book of fiction or non-fiction may be borrowed, and not more than four supplementary tickets, on each of which one book of non-fiction only may be borrowed.
7. Readers must take great care of books and must protect them in wet weather. Loss or damage to books on loan to the borrower must be paid for at the cost of replacement or re-binding, whichever the Librarian considers necessary.
8. The borrower should point out to the Librarian any defect, defacement or damage which he notices in any book.
9. Books are issued for fourteen days and must be returned on or before the last date stamped on the date label in the book. Should the borrower wish to have the book for a further period, the Librarian will redate it, unless it is otherwise required. Books kept in excess of the time allowed are subject to a fine of 2d. a week, or part of the first week, and 3d. per week or part of each subsequent week, on each volume.
10. Borrowers' tickets are available at any of the Guildford branch libraries, but books must be returned to the branch whence they were taken.
11. In cases of infectious illness in the household, the books must not be returned to the library. The Librarian must be informed and the books taken to the Public Health Department.
12. Change of address must be notified, without delay, to the branch at which the borrower originally registered.
13. The Librarian has discretion to refuse books to any borrower.

ARTIFICIAL AIDS IN MOUNTAINEERING

Artificial Aids
in
Mountaineering

GEOFFREY SUTTON

Published under the auspices of
the Mountaineering Association by

NICHOLAS KAYE
LONDON

First published by
Nicholas Kaye Ltd,
194-200 Bishopsgate, London, E.C.2.
1 9 6 2

Copyright © 1962 Nicholas Kaye Limited
*This book may not be reproduced in whole
or in part without permission.   Application with regard to any use of any part of
this volume should be addressed to the
publishers*

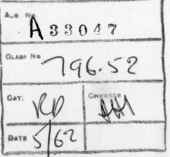
GUILDFORD
PUBLIC LIBRARY

ACC No. A 33047

CLASS No. 796.52

CAT: RD   CHECKED

DATE 5/62

Printed in England by
Wakefield Express Series, Limited
Express House, Southgate
Wakefield.

This publication is approved by The Mountaineering Association as the Teaching Manual of its instructors for modern methods.

NOTE: The following terms are completely interchangeable and have been used quite indiscriminately in this book to avoid monotony—

Abseil = Rappel = Rope down
Duvet=Down (as in sleeping-bag)
Karabiner = Mousqueton = Snaplink
Peg = Piton

CONTENTS

LIST OF ILLUSTRATIONS

INTRODUCTION

Although nothing in the history of mountaineering has caused more controversy than artificial methods, it has always been found a little difficult to define just what an "artificial" method is. The word has meant many different things at various times and places, and what has been considered artificial by one generation has been accepted as natural by the next. The use of crampons provides an example: they were considered unorthodox to the point of heresy by the old guard in the closing decades of the last century, yet to-day they seem as natural and desirable as the ice-axe or the rope itself. If the doctrine of man's unaided powers against the mountain is carried to its logical conclusion, then axe, rope, crampons, special boot soles and protective clothing must all go overboard, and we are left with the ridiculous prospect of a puny naked man shivering his way over the glaciers and on to the rocks without pleasure or prospect of victory. Throughout the ages man, neither the strongest nor swiftest of animals, has won what he has by the use of his brain — to create artificial methods of living. For the purposes of this essay the phrase "artificial methods" may be defined as exactly what it conjures up in the mind of the average climber in 1962, that is the use of pitons and the various techniques connected with them.

When pitons were first seriously introduced those who were jealous of the traditions of the sport, or who felt that their use would ultimately cause a loss in technique or in human values, opposed them with every means at their command. Their point of view, today a lost cause, must be considered with sympathy, and the fact must be faced that they were at least half right even if their opinions were frequently supported by abuse of a kind that seems surprising coming from such rarefied spirits. Where pitons are used too freely it is true that the technique of free climbing suffers; yet it is often true too that those who are best at one are best at the other, and undoubtedly many of the finest climbs would not be possible without them. At the same time those who felt that progress, including exploration, could only go on with the new aids, were equally zealous in their defence. The arguments of their opponents were compromised, perhaps irrelevantly, by the fact that very few of them had ever put themselves into a position where they might have been called upon to use one. Meanwhile the younger climbers, who quietly went on climbing while the battle raged over their heads, began to use them increasingly, and so the battle was in reality lost and won almost before it had started — although that did not cause it to lose any of its bitterness.

Like many other continental movements the change came late to conservative England. The idea of hammering spikes into otherwise unclimbable rock is a pretty obvious one, and had of course occurred to some of the pioneers, and even to other men who for one reason or another needed to surmount rocks long before the sport of climbing had been born. The very occasional use of pegs is recorded in the earlier annals of mountaineering, for example on the first descent of the Hirondelles ridge of the Grandes Jorasses in 1911: but pitons in something approaching their modern form were first used in the Limestone Alps of Bavaria and Austria in the years just preceding the 1914 war. Dulfer, Plank and others began to use them on their routes in the Karwendel and Kaisergebirge, on the Fleischbank, Christaturm, Totenkirchl and other cliffs, both for protection and eventually some direct aid. After the war the fashion spread to the Dolomites, and Solleder opened up the first Grade VI climb on the Civetta, on which eleven pitons were used. The rock in the Eastern Alps is particularly suitable for pegging, and many of the faces are unclimbable without it. As these were attempted the fashion spread, karabiners were introduced, and techniques evolved for traversing and descent. Some of those accustomed to the new techniques visited the Western Alps, and routes like the North face of the Matterhorn (1931) and the South ridge of the Aiguille Noire de Peuterey (1930) began to appear: between the two wars almost all the great new routes in the Western Alps were put out by climbers who had developed their technique in the Eastern. This might be termed the era of free climbing with pegs. In 1933 Comici inaugurated a new approach by his ascent of the North face of the Cima Grande di Lavaredo, with its initial 800ft. overhang, which necessitated the all-out use of rope tension and stirrups over a major part of the climb for the first time. In 1935 Cassin climbed the still harder and more artificial Cima Ovest, where before him twenty-seven strong parties had failed, and the following year even more difficult and grandiose faces were climbed on the Marmolada and Valgrande. These climbs were harder and more "modern" than anything the West had to show at that time. The same was true on ice: the technique of artificial aids on ice had been developed on the North faces of Tyrol and other parts of Austria by Ertl and others. When these men "went West" the various last problems fell before their new methods in a way which astonished the more traditional climbers of Britain and France and Switzerland: on ice the great successes of Welzenbach on the North faces of the Grands Charmoz (1931), Dent D'Hérens (1925) and the Lauterbrunnen North faces in the early '30s: on mixed terrain the German parties on the Eigerwand (1938) and the Croz spur of the Grandes Jorasses (1935): and on rock the epic climbs of Cassin (the North faces of the Piz Badile, the Aiguille de Leschaux, and the Walker spur on the Jorasses, nearly all done in bad weather) and of Ratti on the West face of the Aiguille Noire, and of Gervasutti (the south face of the Punta Gugliermina, the Pillars of Fresnay and the East face of the Grandes Jorasses).

Yet even on these climbs, which contained artificial pitches of considerable difficulty, the climbing was still fundamentally "free". The artificial parts formed a lesser proportion of the whole than in the Eastern Alps and though the Western climbs were higher, longer, and perhaps more serious, they were less difficult technically. After the 1939 war the French suddenly came into the field with a rush, and they and the Italians forced the last and steepest faces, some of which, like the East face of the Grand Capucin de Tacul (Bonatti and Ghigo, 1951) and the West face of the Dru (Berardini, Dagory, Lainé and Magnone 1952) required artificial climbing on the Eastern scale for hundreds of feet at a time, so that several days and nights had to be passed on the climb, and bivouacs passed suspended from pitons on stirrups. Since then even more difficult and sustained routes have been made, both in the Eastern and Western Alps. Expansion bolts have begun to be used. As the amount of equipment necessary has increased, weight has become a serious problem. On the new super direct routes on the Tre Cime di Lavaredo, the original parties left their food and bivouac gear in sacks on the ground, attached to them by hundreds of feet of line, so that they could haul it up in the evening and lower it back again by day. All this activity has led to much refinement of technique, which it is hoped to present in the pages which follow.

The almost complete eschewal of artificial aids by British climbers until 1951 has meant that since 1920 their place in Alpine exploration has been negligible. There is nothing to be proud of in such a record, but happily since 1951 the bonds of tradition have been loosened and there are signs of a rejuvenation. And to do ourselves justice, tradition has not been the only reason for our ignorance. The rock in Wales and the Lake District is perfect for free climbing but ill adapted in general to artificial work—which is just the opposite to some parts of the Alps. And it is a fact that this concentration on getting up cracks without pitons or wedges has led to a higher standard of crack

14

climbing in this country than elsewhere. It is only lately that climbers have begun to use the limestone crags of Derbyshire, Yorkshire and Somerset, which are well-suited to pegging.

But quite often the point is not the actual impossibility of a move, but that on an Alpine face 3,000ft. high there simply is not time to spend hours working out each move or plucking up nerve, and the climber with doubtful security, poised on minute holds on a vertical dolomite cliff does not feel like adventuring too far from the possibility of a rest or retreat or protection. Certain faces cannot be climbed without artificial means, and if we consider them worth climbing at all we must use the necessary techniques. Certainly no one can be considered a completely sound mountaineer who has not a thorough acquaintance with them.

The argument for and against can be carried on endlessly with much justice on both sides, but one thing is sure: pitons have come to stay. It is up to the individual's sporting instinct when they are to be used, and when not. The best modern climbers employ them very sparingly and only as a last resort in the minimum numbers possible. Only third-rate men scatter them around indiscriminately where they have not been used before. If a personal opinion may be offered as a rough guide, I would suggest that they can reasonably be used as belays whenever there is no natural one that will definitely hold the party if the leader falls: for further protection and assistance whenever one was used on the first ascent: to save one's life if a fall is imminent or an irreversible and hopeless position has been reached: and that once a piton is in it is legitimate to use it in any way one's intelligence may suggest. On first ascents judgment has to be brought into play, especially on loose rock (a larger number of pegs is probably permissible on limestone than on granite, for instance), but it is to be remembered that in Britain there is no credit in getting up a piece of rock with ten or even two pitons if someone else can come along, even in ten years' time, and do it without any. It must be emphasized that pitons are not designed to bring Very Severe climbs within the range of climbers whose true standard is lower. By using pitons to get up them they have not turned themselves into V.S. leaders, they have brought the climb down to their own standard. A good example of this sort of abuse is the frequent insertion of a piton in the wall of "Slape" climb on Clogwyn y Grochan in North Wales. In the Alps a good deal more latitude is allowable, but for the good of the sport some sense of restraint should be retained.

For the sake of completeness the technique of drills and rawlplugs is covered in this article. These have been used for many years in the U.S.A. and Spain, but have only recently been needed in the Alps. A few climbs have also been done with their aid on limestone crags in this country. They have made possible some remarkable routes: for example, the 650ft. South face of the Cavall Bernat near Barcelona required nine days and 71 bolts. Indiscriminate use of these aids would obviously be even more meritless than indiscriminate use of pitons, but fortunately the sheer tedium and hard work they entail makes their widespread abuse unlikely. There are no hard and fast limits to these things: the rules are arbitrary, personal and changing, no more than a matter of taste. In 1962 anybody who used a bolt anywhere but on limestone would be laughed out of court, and even on limestone except on new routes or where they had been used before.

The pleasure of artificial climbing largely resides in the remarkable situations and positions it enables one to attain. Those who are fond of the strenuous type of free climbing will probably enjoy it, those who prefer delicacies will not. As with other branches of sport some people have a natural aptitude for it; apart from strength and endurance they have a kind of eye for possibilities and solutions. All in all, it can be safely stated that artificial climbing is easier than free: at any rate the hardest free routes get done a lot less often than the hardest artificial. It must also be noted that whereas a free pitch will normally retain its absolute standard of difficulty, an artificial pitch gets easier as more pitons are left in it until it is completely pegged. The difference between a first and a fortieth ascent is much greater on an artificial climb than on a free one. This is very far from saying that all artificial climbs eventually become easy.

So far I have written almost entirely of rock. This work also contains a section on snow and ice. Once the angle of a snow or ice slope genuinely approaches the vertical some form of attachment to the slope becomes necessary if the climber is to retain his balance, and over the vertical he needs something definite to pull up on. The difficulty depends very much on the texture of the surface, but is naturally greater, and the security is often less, than in classical ice-work. These means are seldom employed for more than a short pitch or so at a time, such as the overcoming of a schrund, a cornice, or a bar of seracs. Such a pitch can be very satisfying, but if the angle continues without a break beyond one rope's length great difficulty will be found in arranging for a tolerable stance, and in practice it is very rare to find anything so long. Things may change in the future, but in 1962 anyone who found himself committed to more than one such pitch in close succession would be asking himself if he had chosen the best route. Once again the technique was invented in the Eastern Alps and has been carried to its highest development there. Its use is comparatively rare; and of course the conditions on ice-faces are extremely variable, so that what requires pitons and tension one year may be cramponned up without step-cutting three or four years later. Artificial ice-pitches have been climbed not only in the Alps but in the Andes (South face of Aconcagua), Himalayas (Kangchenjunga), and Caucasus (South face of Ushba) since about 1925. Ice-axes have of course been forced into vertical snow and used to overcome schrunds and cornices ever since ice-axes were invented.

It is hoped that the present work will form a handy and fairly complete work of reference to the subject.

EQUIPMENT

1. Rope

(a) Material

The ideal rope for artificial climbing would unite a number of characteristics which are not in fact to be found combined in any rope existing in 1962. It should be easy to grip, easy to pull through karabiners, remain manageable in all weather conditions, be light, strong, and not stretchy. It should be noted that what is ideal for artificial climbing may not be so for free, a drawback which applies to all kinds of equipment. Since both kinds of climbing are frequently encountered on the same ascent, and since only one lot of kit can be carried on account of the vital weight-factor, the rope will have to represent a compromise. Let us therefore consider the various types of rope in order to decide which is best.

Hemp is the easiest to grip and the cheapest. It is still favoured by some Dolomite climbers. But its large diameter makes it awkward to clip in or to pull through a number of karabiners, while the thinner varieties are not strong enough. It is difficult to keep and does not last long. Finally its bad weather characteristics of getting wet, kinking, freezing, jamming, getting heavy and becoming generally unmanageable rule it out completely for mountain use wherever nylon or similar material is available and an economic possibility. Much the same applies to flax. However, on outcrops the cheapness of hemp may make it desirable to many. Climbing ropes should never be tarred.

Grass ropes are unsuitable on account of their total lack of resilience. Cotton is pointless because of much better alternatives. Silk ropes are now so rare that they can safely be left out of the question, though their properties might be worth reinvestigating.

We are left with the artificial fibres such as nylon, perlon and terylene. For purposes of artificial climbing they can be considered identical. Nylon is impermeable, so that it does not get soaked, frozen or unmanageable in bad weather. It is easy to store, and lasts a long time without use; but it frays easily, and as it is expensive it is wasteful to use it on small outcrops, especially for top-roping. In heavy use its durability is fair. Its elasticity and resilience give it great resistance to shock-loadings such as falls, but are something of a drawback in artificial work because half the work of the second man pulling may be absorbed in the stretch of the rope. Also its smoother texture and smaller diameter, though enabling it to slide more easily through karabiners, make it less easy for the second man to grip. For a given strength it is very much lighter than hemp. For free climbing whether on snow or rock, it is far superior. Its advantages infinitely outweigh its drawbacks, and I have no hesitation in saying that in 1962 nylon is the best material for all kinds of climbing ropes.

(b) Form

There are two main types of nylon rope, the braided and the laid. The braided kind is only braided on the surface, the inner fibres running straight down the middle (and, like all nylon fibres, the full length of the rope). The surface is consequently smooth and slides easily through karabiners. As there is no twist there is less tendency to kink, and the elasticity is less. This of course means that initially it is slightly weaker than a laid rope, but for the sort of strains involved in artificial climbing it is more than sufficient, and the smoothness and relative lack of stretch are an advantage from the point of view of transmitting the pull of the second man to the leader. These ropes last longer and fray less easily than laid ones. After a certain amount of use, the plaited rope is actually stronger than the laid. Owing to its smoothness the slight initial strength and "gripability" penalty of the plaited sort can be overcome by using

20

a slightly thicker diameter without detriment to its running qualities through karabiners, but then of course the penalty of extra weight has to be paid. Unfortunately these cords are more expensive than laid ones, and anyway are not at present made in Britain, so that they are out of the question for the majority of British climbers. From an all-round point of view they are superior for mountaineering to the laid ones. This does not mean that the laid are not perfectly good enough for the job. Artificial climbs of all grades have been done with them with complete satisfaction, and on the scores of price and availability they are to be recommended.

(c) Colour

Artificial climbing is a strenuous business and where a long stretch of it is foreseen it is highly desirable that every move should be as fast and effortless as possible. The drill is greatly facilitated if the two ropes connecting leader and second are of different colours. The benefits will be particularly appreciated when the ropes are twisted through a number of karabiners, or when the leader is out of sight of his second round a corner or over an overhang. "Take in red, slack white" is easier to say and do than "Take in . . . no, not that one: look out, you're pulling me off, slack it off . . . not all at once, stupid . . . now, which one was it? . . ." and so on. Remembering that a long rope will be needed for abseiling and that the middle should be marked, the author is of the opinion that it is better to use one long rope doubled, of which each half is a different colour, than two separate ropes — because the knot between them is apt to catch when the abseil is pulled down. If coloured ropes cannot be obtained it is possible to dye them oneself with nylon dye, which should be fixed with acetic acid (vinegar). It is probably as well to do the boiling in a double cooker so that the nylon does not come into direct contact with flame-heated metal.

21

(d) Diameter

The thicker diameters are easier to grip and harder to stretch, and of course they are safer and last longer, but these advantages are counterbalanced by their weight, expense, draw, and the difficulty of getting them through the gate of a karabiner that is already full of ropes. It is really a matter of choice between "full-weight" and "three-quarter" nylon, each having a lot to be said for it. In greater mountaineering the author's personal preference is for three-quarter, mostly on the vital score of weight. The sacks are already heavy enough in all conscience, and time is a key-factor.

(e) Length

Whether one or two ropes are used, whatever the fibre or diameter of the rope, there should be not less than 100ft. between each man. For abseiling in the Alps a 200ft. rope is a minimum; and 240ft., though more of a handful, will often make it possible to reach more comfortable stances whether going up or down. Some climbers even use 300ft., but this is rarely strictly necessary and the weight and expense have to be considered—though it does make possible very rapid descents and retreats. The author would recommend 200ft. as sufficient to parties finding their way, and if later they feel the need for something longer they will already be experienced enough to know how much they want. On a steep continuous pitch, especially if the rope runs round any corners or roof overhangs, it frequently becomes impossible to move against the drag of the rope after about 15 pitons have been clipped into, and this may give less than 80ft.

The best equipment for all-round mountaineering including serious artificial work would be a 240ft. plaited nylon three-quarter with each half a different colour, and a 120ft. laid nylon three-quarter for sack-haulage. As plaited rope is hard to get hold of a laid rope is a perfectly good alternative.

2. Pitons

There are a great many sizes and shapes of pitons designed to go into different types of crack. Let us dispose at once of the belief that different pegs are needed for vertical than for horizontal cracks. A moment's thought will show that either can be used for either but it will also show that pitons on which the ring is at right-angles to the blade (i.e. the *horizontal* sort) are more practical, for if the others are hammered into a right-angled corner along one wall it is impossible to put a karabiner on them. Pitons can be of either soft or hard metal, and which is more useful will depend on the type of rock: in general the softer the rock the harder the piton, and vice-versa. Normally the best material is a fairly mild steel that will bend and shape itself into a crack, and the peg should be cadmiumised. The ring should be at a right-angle to the blade, be robust enough to resist the shock of a man falling, and big enough to take at least two karabiners.

It is a good thing to find out what kind of pitons a climb requires most of before doing it, and to carry a preponderance of them, but it is always wise to have a bit of a selection. Three or four basic types can be distinguished, on which there are innumerable variations.

Pegs with a plain blade. See Fig. 1 (a). These may be from 3 to 12 centimetres long, and from 2 to 10 millimetres thick, the shortest usually being the thinnest. The very short and thin ones are called "ace of hearts" and are not needed very often on granite. On limestone it is worth having one or two about. The next size are called "extra-plat" by the French, usually just "thin" by ourselves, and are often useful. Then come the more ordinary models, often about 8 centimetres long and four millimetres thick at the base. We usually just refer to these as "blade" or "ordinary blade." Sometimes one sees very big blades, but they have tended to be replaced by

23

(b) Channel pegs. The cross-section of the blade has the form of a flattened U. They are used in wider cracks, and vary from 5 to 25 millimetres in thickness at the base of the blade, and from 5 to 20 centimetres in length. Once fully in they grip magnificently. See Fig. 2 (b);

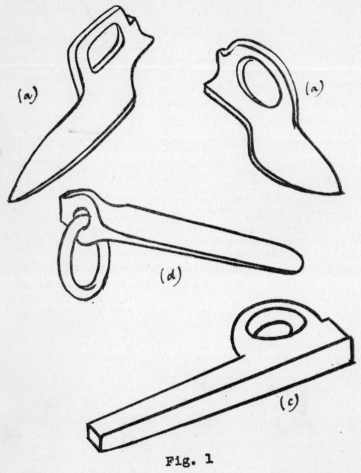

Fig. 1

(c) Another kind of peg for use in wide cracks is made of soft light alloy. They usually have a blunt tapering blade, are about 8 or 9 centimetres long, and taper off from a thickness of from 10 to 20 millimetres. Their gripping power is the most astonishing of all, and they will sometimes hold a man's weight when only half an inch or so into an upside-down crack. See Fig. 1 (c).

(d) A further type is the blade peg with movable ring. Though quite adequate for ordinary purposes they are probably less strong than the fixed-ring kind, and their particular use is in descent, when they make it possible to abseil direct from them without leaving any sling or karabiner behind. See Fig. 1 (d).

(e) Then there are ice-pegs. These are never less than 8 inches long, and are better if they are longer, up to a foot or so. The ring may be movable or fixed, but in either case should hang downwards when the peg is in flat side horizontal. The form can be a flat blade (see Fig. 2, e^2), which is perhaps the best in snow and is certainly the best for carrying in the hand as a climbing-dagger, but is inclined to split ice. The edges of the blade are usually barbed or serrated. Or the peg can be a long channel-section or a tube (see Fig. 2, e^1), preferably slotted so that the ice can freeze through it. The author favours the tubular ones in snow-ice because they do not split it, they freeze in and grip well, and can easily be got out by twisting. They also break less easily. Almost anything seems to split or chip water-ice and nothing feels very firm in it, but perhaps tubes are best. A new development is ice-screws. These are pitons with a thread on them which can be screwed in and out of the ice. The author has no personal experience of them, but they are said to be a tremendous improvement on very steep or overhanging surfaces. Obviously the texture of the snow-ice would need to be reasonably firm, but not more so than with ordinary ice-pegs. In Switzerland yet another technique has been used for the descent of steep ice-faces: the party carries a brace and bit of fairly large diameter, and into the holes so bored stout bamboo stakes are inserted which are then used as abseil points.

3. Wedges

Where artificial aid is required and the cracks are too big for pitons, wooden wedges are used instead. Ash is the best wood, and failing ash, something of a

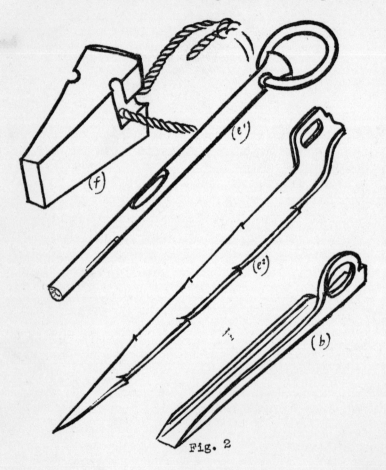

Fig. 2

similar hardness and texture—the wood must be hard enough to withstand heavy hammering, yet soft enough to grip well. The wedges may be any size, but will not normally be any smaller than a very thick piton or bigger than 6in. long, 3in. wide, and 4in. thick at the thick end, tapering perhaps 1½in. in their length. A hole is bored through the thick end through which a short length of nylon line is threaded and knotted into a ring. Grooves should run from the hole to the thick end of the wedge so that the wedge can be driven right home without the sling getting damaged. See Fig. 2 (f).

4. Piton Hammers

These are very various in design, but the important thing is that they should be very stout and have plenty of weight in the head. The shaft may be reinforced near the head with strips of metal, rather in the manner of an ice-axe, and it is a good thing to look for this. A hole should be drilled through the lower end of the shaft so that a length of line can be threaded through it to use as an attachment to the body. The method of attachment favoured by most of the leading climbers is a loop big enough to go over the head and one shoulder. A single thickness of line connects this loop with the hammer. It is important for the sling to be long enough for the hammer to be used at full stretch. It is easiest to carry the hammer when not in immediate use in a rule pocket in the side of the right breeches leg. Some prefer to use a large patch hip-pocket for the purpose.

The head itself can either be shaped like a mallet, flat at both ends, which is good enough where not much snow or ice is expected: or it can have a small pick at one end, and if use in high mountains is anticipated this form is to be preferred. See Fig. 3 (g). The pick is good for gardening and for clearing verglas, and on expeditions where a small amount of glacier and a large amount of severe rock makes the weight of an ice-axe undesirable it does valuable duty as an axe itself. On big North faces, where the ice and the

27

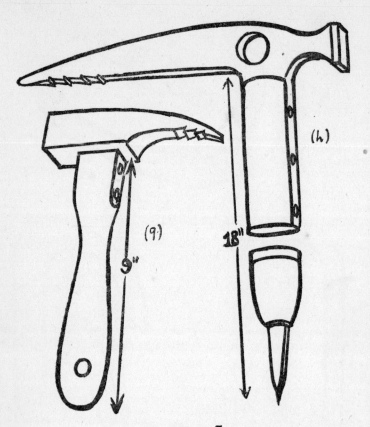

(h)

(g)

9"

18"

Fig. 3

rock get very mixed up and weight is important, a
cross between a piton-hammer and an ice-axe is sometimes used which is the size of a very small axe and
has a pick but a hammer instead of the adze. See Fig.
3 (h).

If the occasional security peg is all that is expected
a light hammer will be sufficient, but for genuine artificial climbing the hammer should be heavy. The

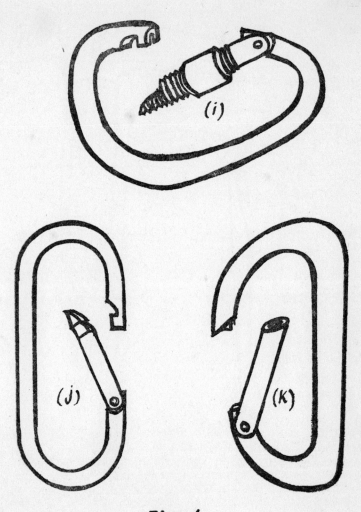

Fig. 4

weight reduces the number of blows needed for each piton and thereby saves a great deal of energy. A generous striking area on the head is also an asset.

5. Karabiners

Also known as mousquetons and snaplinks, or more familiarly, "krabs." The larger the karabiner, the more convenient it is. But against this we have to set the weight factor, all-important when anything up to twenty karabiners may have to be carried by a party of two: indeed, this is often the heaviest item of all. We prefer them large so that with a couple of étriers and a rope clipped in there will still be plenty of room for the hand to grip. Karabiners for pegging do not need to be as strong as for running belays and waist-loops, because if a fall occurs it is usually very short and the strain therefore not high (owing to the frequency of the pitons: normally the only reason for a fall on artificial climbs is a piton coming out unexpectedly). For this reason we can compensate for the increased size by making them of light alloys. The catch on the gate of ordinary karabiners is a great nuisance because it engages when the karabiner is in tension (as, for example, when someone is standing in an étrier which is clipped into it) and so makes it difficult to open the gate in order to manoeuvre the ropes. Because strength is not the only objective it is quite in order to have no catch on the gate, and it is more convenient without. It also saves a lot of skin and strength in the fingers if the spring on the gate be weak and easily worked, and a wide gate makes the insertion and extraction of ropes much easier. The big D-shaped karabiners would be ideal but for their weight and the gate screw and catch, and are very handy for carrying pitons (see Fig. 4 (i)). The screw-up type have no particular application to artificial work. The normal kind we use so much for running belays in this country are quite adequate to any artificial work, but not ideal on account of the catch and the weight. See Fig 4 (j). A word of warning should, however, be added against W.D. karabiners,

30

The descendeur (m) is
discussed on Page 37

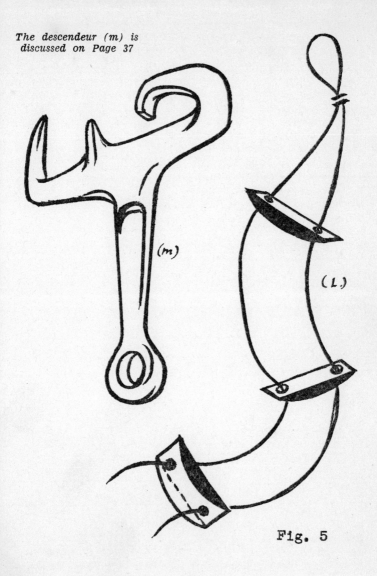

(m)

(L)

Fig. 5

which are dangerous. The author has seen one of these open after a leader's fall of only three feet, and cut the rope into the bargain. The varying types of oddly shaped karabiners one sees from time to time have no particular advantage, and certainly the best sort of karabiner yet produced for artificial climbing, whether on rock or ice, is the alloy model made in Paris. Fig. 4 (k).

Perhaps the ideal outfit for a big artificial climb would include a couple of screw-up karabiners for attachment and abseiling purposes, a couple of D-shapes for carrying pegs, and 12 or 16 alloys for the climbing. In practice most of us can only afford a limited number which have to serve for all purposes, and in this case a mixed bag usually results. But on a big route the weight and convenience factors cannot be over-emphasised. Our outfit must depend on our ambitions.

6. Etriers

Authorities seem to differ on the subject of étriers (See Fig. 5 (1)): the Italians, for example, go in for big ones of several rungs, whereas the French rarely use more than two-rung ones. Each climber will develop his own preferences and make his own stirrups accordingly. Nevertheless a few suggestions may be found useful. The best material for the rope part is plaited Terylene, which can be obtained from yachting stores. It is impermeable like nylon but less stretchy, and being plaited it does not kink. The rungs are best made of metal for strength, and should be at least 1in. across (so that they stand out slightly when lying against the rock, thus enabling a toe to be got on to them, and so that they are tolerably comfortable to sit or stand on) and at least 5in. wide. Tubular rungs, cut-up broomstick handles, or rope rungs are unsatisfactory for the same reasons. The top of the étrier should be tied into a small loop with a figure of eight knot, and wrapped round with adhesive tape. The distance of the first rung below this, and of each successive rung will be a matter of taste and build.   The author likes each gap to be about 18in. The number of rungs is likewise optional, the majority of British climbers (including the author) favouring three.   The rungs should be supported by knots, but there should be no knot above the rung (contrary to at least one opinion that has appeared in print) or it will be impossible to slide it up to make room for the knee on overhangs. A good knot for this purpose is the figure of eight knot. If the ends of line left under the bottom rung are left sufficiently long, they can be tied together, thus forming a small loop which will be found handy when (as quite often happens, especially in de-pegging) it is desired to clip one étrier to the bottom of another. One of the most strenuous aspects of artificial climbing is constantly having to move up and down recuperating étriers from the pegs below and clipping them on above. This can be completely avoided by the use of "Fifi-hooks," a technique that has come in the last two or three years. A steel hook is attached to the étrier (see illustration) and from the top of its bend a line goes to the climber's waist.   The manner of use is described under the appropriate heading: suffice it to say here that it is far and away the best method of artificial, and will no doubt become universal. Each climber should carry three étriers and one "cow's tail," a loop of rope attached to the waistloop and clipped in to the pitons successively at waist level as one moves up, thus avoiding much strain to one's partner.   The author likes the loop short, but perhaps the best plan is to make it with a Tarbuck knot so that it is adjustable.

7.   Expansion Bolts

The outfit necessitates a star drill, which should have some form of attachment to the body. The bolts themselves can be of various designs, but the type normally used in the building trade is probably as satisfactory as any. A size large enough for reasonable strength should be chosen, but it must be remembered that the larger the bolt the longer the hole for it will take to bore. A spanner is needed to tighten up the bolt. Hangers, each consisting of a plate of bent metal with a hole in each plane, one to slip on to the bolt and lie flat against the face, the other to stand out at an angle and receive a karabiner, are also required in numbers equal to the karabiners carried. These are secured on with a nut. Some kinds of bolt can be taken out and used again, others become permanent fixtures. The former are both stronger and in the long run cheaper. Ordinary screws and fibre rawlplugs work quite well for limited strains. Recently a model has come on the market in form resembling a short piton with a split cylindrical blade, in which a small wedge is ready inserted. When the peg is hammered in the wedge expands it. This is the most convenient form yet, and no hanger is needed.

8. Clothing and Footwear

Ordinary vibram-soled boots or kletterschuhe are the best footwear. Nails are totally unsuitable and even dangerous, and rubbers soon become intolerably hard on the feet when standing in étriers. Note that eyes or D-rings are better than hooks as a method of doing up the boots, as the latter are inclined to catch on étriers. Ordinary climbing breeches are best, and useful features include a rule pocket in the right leg to hold the hammer, and a very large hip-pocket. Since no one wears braces when climbing nowadays I scarcely need add that a belt and a snug-fitting waist is better. Other clothing is pretty well normal and to taste, but should be stout and include a pair of gloves. The anorak needs a good front-pocket, and for Alpine work a down (duvet) jacket is almost essential.

9. Rucksack and Bivouac Equipment

Many big artificial climbs necessitate one or more bivouacs, so a word may be permitted on the subject. Containing food, spare clothing and climbing "swag," the sack is likewise a vital item. It should be designed not only to be worn but to be hauled. It must therefore be of very stout canvas, have as few pockets and projections as possible (a waist-strap and simple attachments for axe and crampons are, however, desirable) and be fitted at the top with a very firmly attached metal ring into which a karabiner can be clipped for hauling. A leather base may perhaps be rejected on grounds of weight, but lined leather shoulder straps are desirable, and they should be detachable at the bottom by means of a spring catch—not a simple hook. Pegs are always making holes, and if the sack is to last long these should be patched as soon as they appear. If it can be rubberised or waterproofed so much the better: if not a plastic bag may be used for a lining to contain clothing and food and fuel. If the sack is made in the form of a tube about four feet long half of it can be folded down into itself when it is in use as a sack (in which case the drawcord should run through "belt-loops" on the outside at mid-height) and for the bivouac it can be unfolded and pulled over the legs to the waist, affording vital protection in bad weather and obviating the need to carry a separate pied d'elephant. A down jacket is almost essential, and should include a hood. A short down bag reaching just to the waist is a borderline case, its desirability depending on circumstances. A light waterproof tent-sack or a plain sheet of plastic large enough to pull right over and round the party completes the outfit. One might perhaps add a pair of spare socks. Such an outfit is quite light and with normal toughness on the part of the climber will enable most nights to be sat out in safety if not in comfort. This of course refers to Alpine altitudes. In the Dolomites it may be reasonable to carry less, in the Andes or Himalayas obviously a good deal more will be required, but in all cases the object is to carry the minimum consistent with safety. If a bivouac on snow is in prospect it would probably be sensible to have a light aluminium shovel for digging in, and an air-cushion: if the prospect is a bivouac in étriers then some form of seat could be considered.

If there is any water in the face at all, the weight of a water-bottle can be avoided by carrying a thin piece of rubber tube through which it can be readily sucked up. While actually climbing, thirst (which can become very strong during a long session of artificial climbing) can be allayed by a good supply of acid-drops, which again is lighter and more convenient than a water-bottle. On a climb of more than one day it is important not to become dehydrated. Dehydration seems to cause fatigue and loss of morale.

Cooking, in other words chiefly hot drinks, will be done on a light alloy spirit or Meta cooker, one of which is enough for a party, because the longer one can spin out the cooking on a bivouac the better: it keeps the mind off the cold.

Food depends on individual taste. Pain d'épices is invaluable because it is light, filling, nutritious, digestible, and does not go stale. It is normally only obtainable in France. Fruit cake and parkin are good substitutes, but hard to come by abroad. A little butter helps these down and is good for one. Hot sweet drinks containing plenty of sugar (tea, cocoa, etc.), are essential, and packet soups light and acceptable. A small twist of salt is perhaps worthwhile because cramp is a great enemy on very long climbs. Eggs, bacon, meat pâte, jam, are all worth considering according to taste, plus perhaps some bread for filling purposes (kept in a plastic bag) and plenty of acid drops, chocolate and sugar. Fruit is heavy and squashable, yet a great morale-raiser. Once again it must be repeated, however, that lightness must be sought ruthlessly.

A very light head-torch will be felt to be indispensable once its convenience has been experienced. A small flask of brandy or rum makes a good start to the night, and of course smokers will need matches and tobacco. Some kind of waterproof covering should be devised for the matches. Drugs, either sleeping or sustaining, are used by some climbers, but the author favours them only in extreme necessity.

36

10. Methods of Attachment

Once again this will be a matter of taste. One can quite well just tie on to the rope in the usual way. Some continental climbers use a simple shoulder harness or baudrier, which they claim is better in the event of a fall. Some like a loop over the top of one shoulder, and/or a loop under one or both buttocks. The author has always found the normal Tarbuck attachment most satisfactory: a full-weight hemp three times round the waist, to which the ropes are attached, each one separately, by the strongest karabiners on the market. It should be noted that the knotted loops by which the ropes are clipped into the waist-loop karabiners should be very small so that the leader can be pulled as close as possible to his pitons. Many climbers have an extra little loop at their waists which they clip in when not in motion, thus freeing both hands without needing tension from their companion. If operating on a continuously over-hanging face where a fall would suspend the climber clear of the rock, it is prudent to have a prusik loop attached to the rope and pushed into a pocket. It is also prudent to practise using it.

11. The Descendeur

This is a species of three-pronged fork designed to make abseiling easier (See Fig. 5 (m)). The ring on the handle is clipped in to the waist loop or abseiling thigh-loop with a karabiner so that the hooked prong is on the left. The abseil rope is then brought in under the hook and curled twice round the fork. In action the left hand holds the descendeur and the right pays through the rope. For new and unknown descents it will contribute largely to the comfort and security of the party, but otherwise (though the device has fanatical adherents who will disagree) in the opinion of the author it does not begin to justify its admittedly slight weight unless at least half a dozen abseils are foreseen. However, its use does save a great deal of wear on the clothes and also a drenching if the rope is wet. Attachments can also be bought for normal karabiners which have the effect of turning them into descendeurs, but the author's purely personal opinion of these is that they concentrate a great deal of heat at the end of a long abseil on a nylon rope. Perhaps it should be mentioned for completeness that there is also a device called a décrocheur which enables the climber to abseil on a single rope and yet recover the end, but there would seem to be several possible snags.

12. Methods of Lassoing

For certain climbs it is necessary to project a line over a distant spike or pinnacle before this can be reached. This may be done by ordinary cowboy methods, but where the distance is too great crossbows and rockets have been used. The design of these can safely be left to the imagination of the climbers concerned. For any except extraordinary distances a strong catapult will be equally efficient and at the same time lighter and easier to procure. It can be used to fire a metal nut to which a line is attached, which is in turn tied on to a proper rope.

13. Slings

Though we use these mostly in free climbing they can be very handy in artificial too, and it is always worth having two or three about to serve as supplementary hand and footholds, prusik loops, etc., and to thread behind chockstones (see sub-section 15 on chockstones). They should be knotted (not spliced), of nylon of varying thicknesses, and circumference can also be varied, three or four feet being perhaps the most useful, or double the circumference used double. They may have one or two nuts threaded on them as ready-made chockstones.

Among continental climbers it is becoming increasingly common to wear a crash helmet, a precaution which has long been a matter of course among pot-holers (to say nothing of jockeys, racing drivers, motor-cyclists and all others who need to envisage impacts on the head). A light model does not impede as much as the hood of an anorak. Quite apart from the question of falling oneself, a great many excellent climbers have been killed by unpredictably falling stones who would now be alive if they had observed this simple and apparently obvious precaution. It is to be hoped their use will become general among British climbers.

14. Prusik Loops

They can be very useful in case someone falls over an overhang or gets totally stuck on a pitch, whether on rock or ice. Thin slings work well if fairly long and save the weight and complication of separate loops. By the same token it may be worth pointing out that a number of étriers clipped together are an excellent instrument for crevasse-rescue. At least one prusik loop should be attached *before* the possibility of its being needed, for obvious reasons.

15. Chockstones and Jammed Knots

These often make a cheap substitute for pitons or wedges, and ease sensitive consciences into the bargain. The important thing for chockstones is that they should fit the chosen crack accurately and be of hard rock (i.e., gritstone chocks are too friable to be much use, and it is a good idea to import some in the pocket from Wales). Slings threaded behind these natural or inserted chocks can then be used to climb on. A piece of wire often assists threading. They are best inserted in narrowing grooves or above narrow portions of a crack, dropped or pushed in, and worked about until they settle securely. Cracks, which are wider inside than out are particularly suitable. Jammed-knot slings have also been used for direct aid.

The knot should be adapted to the crack and slipped behind a *strangulation*, care being taken that it is well tightened before any strain is put on it. There can be no doubt that such a use of slings and chocks constitutes a form of artificial climbing, and there should be no illusion that the use of a chockstone is in any way more admirable than that of a piton. Reference has already been made to the use of threaded nuts for similar purposes.

16. Crampons

Essential on any steep ice. For artificial work crampons with two points sticking out in front will be an asset. These have until recently been most often seen in the Eastern Alps, but can now be bought at most good dealers.

TECHNIQUE

1. Double Rope Technique

It is often very difficult to say at what point climbing ceases to be free and becomes artificial. Pegs may be put in for protection only: they may be used to pull up and stand on: a little tension may be given in the process: a sling may be used as a footloop: or the whole gamut of pitons, double rope, tension and étriers may be gone through. It will depend on the situation, and quite obviously the quickest solution will be the best. There is no point in wasting time on a high Alpine ridge clipping in an étrier when the move can quite obviously be done without: and equally there is no point in wasting fifteen minutes in the same sort of place trying to do a move clean, when an étrier will obviously solve it in two. A given pitch may often be part free, part artificial. If, therefore, the full-scale artificial process is now described, readers will understand that there is no obligation to use it every time a piton is inserted, and can be relied on to use their own judgment of how much aid a given move will require.

Two men stand at the foot of an overhanging corner. The smooth walls offer little or no hold, the crack is too narrow to jam. The pitch will have to be artificial. (From here on see Fig. 6.) The leader and second tie on to three ropes, a red and a white one for climbing and a third, which will not be clipped through any karabiners, for hoisting the rucksacks. From the leader's waistloop dangle a dozen or so karabiners and a score of pegs (this pre-supposes that pitons are not already in place in the climb) which he has selected out of his sack after examining the average width of the crack. Out of his rule-pocket juts a hammer, the safety sling of which, together with three or four other slings, is round his shoulders. Three étriers, initially tucked over one shoulder, are attached to his waistloop by cords (woven terylene the thickness of a bootlace and perhaps four feet long) from their fifi-hooks. The second man also carries three étriers,

41

a hammer, and a sling or two. Both leader and second have short "cow's-tails" attached to their waistloops.

The second having belayed, the leader goes up to the foot of the crack and hammers in a piton at full stretch, attaches a karabiner to it and then clips in the white rope. He then hooks on an étrier, asks for tension on the white rope and pulls himself up on to the bottom rung where he stands, clips in his cow's tail,

Fig. 6

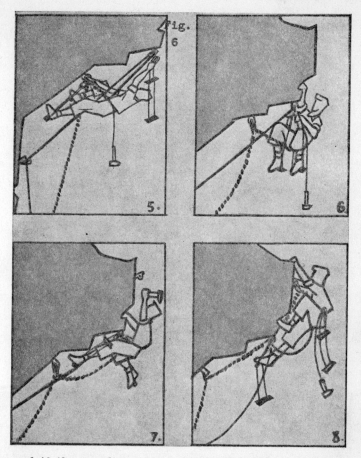

Fig. 6

and if the overhang is pronounced hooks on another étrier against which to balance himself by pushing back with one foot. Two points may be noted here.

(a) The leader is not hoisted up or even held in place by his second. He hoists himself and the cow's-tail holds him. The second gives what help he reasonably can (usually not much) and also, of course, protection.

(b) On very sharp overhangs the strain can be lessened by sitting in an étrier while preparing the next move.

The leader now reaches up, inserts a piton in the crack as far up as possible, and hammers it in. Then he puts on a karabiner, clips in the other rope (i.e. in this case red) and hooks on the third étrier. Then he unclips his cow's tail, tells the second to take in the red, slack off the white, and as this happens he moves up until he is standing on the upper étrier. The two étriers below will by now have detached themselves automatically by the pull of the cords from the waist-loop to the fifis, and they can be drawn up and used in the same way as before. The whole process is now repeated, keeping each rope in as straight a line as possible, and leaving the ropes clipped through the sounder pegs for security. This goes on until a stance is reached or until it becomes possible to dispense with pegs and climb free. The pegs should be as far apart as they can reasonably be put in or as the rock allows. The technique should be practised until it has become an automatic drill, and leader and second understand each other's movements so well that few words are necessary. The order each time is one: peg in, two: clip on rope, three: hook on étrier, four: give word of command, move up, and clip in cow's-tail.

If fifis are not used the étriers are clipped on with karabiners, and in this case it is necessary each time to unclip the one from the peg you have left and put it on the one you are going to next (this used to be the normal method and is shown in the illustrations).

The second now prepares to climb. The process is the same for him except that his pull comes from above, which on overhangs is curiously less helpful than the pull from below, and that he takes out as many of the pegs as he can instead of putting them in. It will often be found that seconding an artificial pitch is more strenuous than leading it. The pull coming from above helps one to move up but does not hold one into the cliff very well. Before removing a

44

peg it is usually necessary to move past it. It is very difficult to hammer effectively at something that is down by one's feet, and seconds may find it helpful to attach one étrier to the foot of another so that they can climb back down to the level of the coveted piton. Note that the second should always unclip his rope from a peg before moving past it. This sounds very obvious but in the heat of the moment people have been known to forget with surprising results.

Two is certainly the best number for a party doing artificial climbing, but if the party consists of three or more then the subsequent members of the party need only be attached by a single rope. As the second goes up he will unclip the leader's rope from the karabiners and put the third man's in its place. The last man carries the second hammer and takes out the pegs.

Continental parties normally trust to the climbing pegs for security and do not use a separate belay. The author, however, is in favour of belaying properly in the usual British manner where possible. The time loss is slight in terms of such work and the security gain for both leader and second is considerable, adding much to pleasure and peace of mind. The easiest way for the second to manage the ropes is probably just one in each hand with a twist over the arm or behind the back, wearing leather gloves. The leader can take in both the second's ropes at once in the usual way round his body. An exception to these rules of security occurs when the length of rope does not permit the leader to reach a stance of any sort, or only the very tiniest stance, so that he is forced to stop and make one in his étriers or on a small foothold. He stops by what he considers a firm peg, ties on to it, seats himself facing the crag in his étrier, puts in another peg and karabiner above his head if possible and takes in the rope through this. If it is not possible to get in another peg it may be necessary to use the peg to which he is already tied. The second can either come up to him or halt on a lower peg, whichever is convenient, and manages the

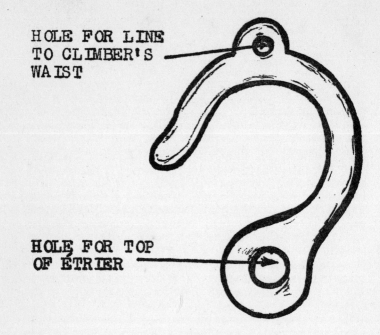

HOLE FOR LINE TO CLIMBER'S WAIST

HOLE FOR TOP OF ÉTRIER

Fifi-hook

Fig. 7

ropes similarly. Any attempt at shoulder or waist belaying in these circumstances causes one to turn upside down.

With experience it becomes possible to tell when a peg is firm enough to be used without knocking it in fully, thus saving time and energy for both leader and second. Every so often it is wise to

46

hammer one right in for security in case of "unzipping." More time and energy will be saved if the following points are noted. Words of command should be simple and clear, e.g., "Take in red, slack white." If the phrase "take in" is always used for taking in the slack, and the word "slack" for paying it out and giving more of it, then in windy weather or around corners the number of syllables can be distinguished even when the words cannot. The other man should be kept informed of what is going on. When tension and slack are asked for the response should be smooth, simultaneous and swift, but not all at once in a jerk.

Two other time-honoured techniques which need no explaining but must be considered artificial are giving a shoulder and using an ice-axe to climb rocks. The latter may be hooked over an obstacle and pulled up on; it may be used to fashion or improve a hold; the pick may be inserted in cracks and twisted so that it forms a secure support (in this case, of course, it is just an inconvenient form of piton) or the shaft may be wedged between chockstones and used as a hold, as on early ascents of the Knubel crack on the Grépon.

2. The Insertion of Pitons

When standing comfortably in balance on a ledge it is an easy matter to reach up and, holding a peg in one hand, knock it in with the other. Usually, however, one has to knock them in while hanging on with one hand, on cramped footholds or perched on a stirrup. It is then very important to choose a peg suitable for the width and depth of the crack, and to choose the best part of the crack for the peg without too much delay. The best place for a piton may quite often be at a widening if the crack is very narrow or choked, and at or above a narrowing if the crack is wide. In horizontal cracks a peg may often be what we call "mechanically sound" for a downward pull even though it is too loose to resist an outward one.

Still holding on with one hand, the leader reaches up and probes until he has found a peg and a bit of crack suitable to each other. He then wedges the peg as firmly as possible, lets go of it altogether to reach down for his hammer, and drives it in as far as it will go. It saves a lot of energy in hammering, as in step-cutting, if the hammer is held by the end of the handle, and the swing of the weight of the head is allowed to do most of the work: this is where the value of a heavy hammer becomes apparent. The security of a piton is judged by the ear and the eye, though it is not a bad plan to give a good testing pull with one's whole weight before committing oneself to a peg about which one is in doubt. As the peg goes in, each blow of the hammer should cause it to sing with a clear musical tone in an ascending scale. When the note is clear and high the peg is firm even though it may not be wholly in or though it is hammered upwards into a roof overhang. A dull, flat sound that does not change as the peg goes home shows that it is not being gripped firmly by the walls of the crack, while a heavy whirring or vibration indicates that the point of the piton has met with some obstruction. However, any fool can use a perfectly sound peg: the finer art comes in making safe progress where it is impossible to get completely sound ones. This is where the eye comes in: it must judge whether a peg is mechanically safe for a pull in a given direction. Thus, as we have already noticed, a peg that would not resist an outward pull may be quite all right for a downward one if it is wedged in a horizontal crack or between two chockstones in a vertical one—though in the latter case a sling would be more in order. If a peg can only be got in for a fraction of its length and no shorter substitute is available we may judge that a pull on the ring at the end of the peg would make it bend and twist out, but that a pull at the point where the peg enters the rock would be safe. The effect can be achieved by hammering the exposed part of the peg down flat against the rock, but this is a wasteful

Fig. 8

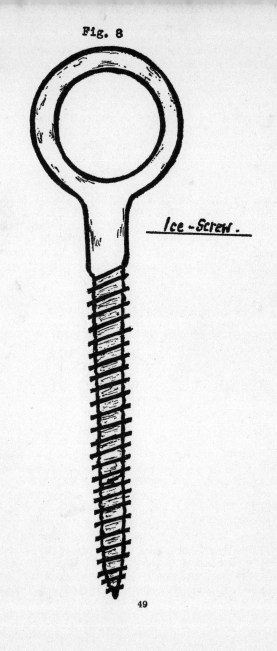

Ice - Screw.

method as it weakens the peg and makes it harder to take out or use again. It also splits channel pegs. The best way is to wind a sling of nylon line a couple of times around the blade where it enters the rock, preferably a short sling, and then attach the karabiner to the sling. A peg in a vertical crack which would not withstand a direct downward pull can often be used safely for a sideways pull such as a layback move, or even for a down-pull if it is inserted so that the pressure will cause it to twist in its crack. This is one of the reasons why pegs with heads set at a right angle to the blade are preferable.

If a peg the right width for a certain crack is not available, it is often possible to drive in two, or even three, side by side so that they jam each other. Or a simple window-wedge may be used to achieve the same effect, being driven in beside the peg.

In wider cracks wooden wedges of various sizes are often used. The technique for inserting them is much the same as for a piton, but there is no singing noise, so that they are best tested carefully by hand before the full weight is committed to them. The subsequent technique is exactly as with pitons, but it is worth keeping in mind that while wedges are excellent for progress they cannot normally be relied on for security.

Pegs that are found in place are best tested briefly before use, and on popular climbs it is polite to leave them where they are found: parties go up expecting to find them and equipped accordingly, and their absence may have serious consequences. On limestone particularly it becomes more difficult to get a secure peg into a given place on each occasion that it is used.

The type of pegs required on a climb will depend quite largely on the type of rock. Hard rocks, such as limestone, gneiss and granite, in general require flexible soft pegs that will shape themselves to the interior of the cracks. Pegging in granite is often strenuous but usually secure, following well-defined cracks and lines of possibility with harder or unclimbable walls and slabs on either side. The cracks, once started, are usually continuous, and if wide are deep, if narrow shallow. It will frequently be worthwhile carrying a good proportion of channel pegs. Limestone is generally looser and less secure, and requires a more refined or inventive technique. The cracks often peter out or close up for distance, but it is sometimes possible to progress up apparently blank walls by means of the little pocks and holes and brief cracks which are a characteristic of this rock. One also occasionally encounters what can best be described as mud-bands, which vary in thickness from a few inches to several feet. These can be very troublesome as nothing sticks in them. It is sometimes necessary to peg behind or beside loose blocks, piled up on each other or jammed in cracks. Extreme cunning and delicacy of touch may be required and really no rules can be laid down about it that are not suggested by common sense. On soft rocks such as sandstone or chalk, hard pegs or iron are generally best. In chalk, it is safest to ignore the cracks and drive the pegs into the bare rock, a dusty and tiresome business. Large portions sometimes split off. Sandstone and grit give pegging similar in character to coarse-grained granite. One quite often runs up against cracks in sandstone which would be suitable for large wedges if they were not climbable clean. Slatey rocks and the various kinds of volcanic rock found in Wales and the Lakes favour soft pegs, but are so adapted that an artificial move is comparatively rarely followed by another in any case. Quartzite is very inconvenient for pegging.

The angle at which pitons enter is not important for progress, provided they are firm. If the singing note is clear and high they can be trusted implicitly even when directly upside-down in roof overhangs. For purposes of arresting falls they are naturally stronger if put in head upwards, however.

To extract a piton simply knock it up and down or from side to side according to the line of the crack until it can be wiggled loose and pulled out by hand. It is not easy for the second man to remove a peg while hanging on to it, and having passed it he will still find it awkward to get at down by his feet. The solution, as we have already had occasion to remark, is to clip an étrier to the bottom of a higher one, thus remaining at the level of the desired peg, but independent of it.

A lot of effort can be wasted or saved according to the technique used for standing in étriers. The object of the exercise all the time is to get as much strain off the hands as possible, both of the leader and second. In corners a lot can be achieved by standing in an étrier with one foot and bridging on the walls with the other foot and back. On less than vertical walls and slabs a foot in an étrier is ample support by itself, but on overhanging walls and above all on roofs every scrap of ingenuity must be mustered to mitigate the strain. It often helps to put two étriers on one peg and press back against one of them with one foot, sometimes in a semi-squatting position. Or, if in a semi-static position, the rung of an étrier can be slid up under one thigh, or even both. The little extra waist-loop sling may come in handy, and a sling is less tiring for the hands to hold on to than a karabiner, especially if the end of it is slid up behind the elbow or under the shoulder.

The pick of the hammer can sometimes be brought into action, when all else fails, to improve a hold or to chip one out where none existed before. This may be especially useful on slabs, where little flakes and pockets can be fashioned into holds by chipping off their tops and excavating their backs, and especially easy on arêtes and big flakes, where the edge can be chipped into incuts.

Perhaps a word should be said about bivouacking. If the bivouac is inevitable it is best to choose a comfortable spot some time before it gets quite dark. The excess baggage can be dumped, the next pitch or two can be climbed and fully equipped with pitons and fixed rope, and the site rejoined by a rappel. The things to look for in a site are roominess, a flat surface, a water supply and an overhanging roof: but in practice the mountains rarely allow us more than a cramped and sloping ledge. Before settling down to cook, shiver and doze each member of the party should belay himself securely, and if the site is really very small or sloping another rope may be fixed across under the arms as a kind of leaning rail. As soon as climbing stops all the spare clothing and bivouac kit should be donned and the boots loosened or, if they are wet, taken off and kept in the sack so they will not freeze. Feet are put into the sack and the rope is used to sit on. The arms are taken out of the sleeves and brought inside across the tummy or chest. A scarf may be used as a loin-cloth. To what extent one sleeps or to what extent one should allow oneself to sleep depends on the site, the weather and our equipment. One should avoid bivouacking on snow if at all possible. Snow should be cleared off bivouac ledges, but if actually caught by darkness on a glacier or ice-climb it will probably be best to continue by torch or moonlight. If this is impossible as large a stance or burrow as possible should be cut out, and if the slope is sufficient an axe or peg belay taken. All the insulation possible will be required to sit on. The possibilities of snow caves (and the comforts of air cushions) have already been mentioned. Snow caves have saved many lives.

It does occasionally happen that people get caught by darkness where there is no site at all. It is then highly desirable to have one or two safe and secure pitons. What happens next will depend on the situation. The classic thing is to sit or stand in êtriers. Perhaps it is preferable to make a kind of cradle by passing the rope a number of times through the karabiner and behind the back and under the seat. The sack could be used for padding. It is important to make quite sure that all vital equipment such as boots, gloves and ironmongery is really secure and cannot fall. In between dozes it is a good thing to keep the circulation going. But the greatest factor of resistance and survival is mental. Do not exaggerate the situation. An attitude of calm determination is best.

3. Descent

The descent of an artificial pitch is effected in the same way as climbing up it except, of course, that everything is in reverse. It is more difficult to insert pitons on the descent, and these pitches will, in fact, normally be descended en rappel. This is quite straightforward and is done in the usual way except when the wall is so overhanging that the rappel rope hangs out clear into space, or when it is not long enough to reach a stance.

In the first case one climber must descend on étriers and doubled rope until he is in plumb-line above the next stance, when, to save time, he can be lowered on to it by the man above. It is important that the upper man should be tied on to the middle of the rope, the lower man to the ends. If there is no stance he must go on climbing down until he reaches his chosen belay piton. In order to sacrifice as few karabiners as possible, he will, in the event of being lowered, leave none above him except the one the lowering rope must run through. If a safety rope is being used it should be left outside this karabiner. The top man pulls up the double rope till it is clear of the karabiner, then rappels on it. He is pulled into the stance by the bottom man with the safety rope.

If there is no safety rope the first man down only clips one of the ropes through the karabiner at the point where he is lowered. He keeps tied on to both ends of the rope. The second man unties and poses the ropes as for a rappel, then rappels on the free strand only, being counterbalanced by his companion on the other rope. The companion is able to pull him to the stance with the end of the free rope, which he has retained. If the stance is on étriers there is no problem as long as the first man does not leave the rope through any of the karabiners above him: the second man simply rappels on the double

54

rope, the end of which is still attached to the first man.

If the rappel rope does not reach any stance but the wall is only vertical so that the end of the rope lies against the rock it is necessary to rope down until a piton (or preferably two) can be inserted on which to make a stance in étriers, and to serve as a point for the next rappel. The nasty business of putting in the peg while hanging on in the rappel position will be greatly eased if a descendeur is used. In effect, if a knot is tied in the rope it blocks the descendeur, and both hands can be removed from the rope to work on the peggery. Alternatively a prusik loop can be attached round both ends of the rappel rope before it is flung down. As in ordinary rappeling it may be necessary to go down diagonally in order to reach the desired place.

4. Traverses

Sometimes we come to blank impossibility, but some yards away to one side is a feasible line which we wish to gain. If this is not possible by free climbing we have to resort to one of the following methods.

The simplest is the pendulum. This simply consists of swinging across on the abseil rope from where we are to where we want to go. Obviously the higher our point of departure in relation to our point of arrival the less of a swing we have to make and the easier the manoeuvre. Sometimes the swing is not sideways but backwards, as in swinging from one pinnacle to another: again, our point of departure should be as high as possible above the point of arrival.

If the traverse has to be horizontal and it is impossible to peg our way across in the normal way with étriers, a few feet can be gained by preparing as for an abseil, with the abseil peg not lower than waist level, though it need not be above the head. Leaning against the drag of the rope and pulling on sideways holds in the other direction a short traverse can be effected. The second man pays out the safety rope carefully according to the leader's instructions, and can make all the difference to the success of the operation. Normally the higher the pegs are above the leader's head the greater the distance that can be gained. This is known as horizontal rappel. The two ends of the rappel rope, which have been pulled after him by the leader, are then fixed and drawn taut so that the second man can come across as on a handrail.

Another method is to lasso some block or spike across where we wish to arrive. This is probably best done if possible with the middle of the rope. Our swing across can be controlled by a rope from the second. Again the rope should be fixed as a handrail for the second, or at least the safety rope should be arranged through a peg or sling at the point of departure, so that his swing can also be controlled. On some rare occasions, to attain an otherwise inaccessible pinnacle, a rope has been shot over with a bow or a rocket. The other end then has to be reached before the traverse can be made by climbing across the rope. While doing this it would be well to clip oneself to it with a sling and karabiner.

5. Ice and Snow

The security of ice-pitons varies enormously with the texture of the surface. Water ice is too hard and brittle: it is dangerous because it splits easily. Snow, even hard snow, is too soft to give such a small thing much security of tenure. They are at their best in snow-ice, where they are trustworthy to quite a high degree. The important thing in putting them in is to make sure that they are at an angle of less than 90 degrees to any strain that is going to be put on them—but not at too sharp an angle, or there will not be a sufficiently thick base of ice under the blade to withstand such a strain. This makes everything quite straightforward until the angle of the slope begins to exceed the vertical. The angle at which the pitons have to be driven in continues to be several degrees above the horizontal, but as the overhang becomes more pronounced the base of ice beneath them becomes progressively thinner, and this at the very time when the potential strains are increasing. The necessity of making quite sure of the quality of the ice before embarking on an overhanging pitch is apparent at once, and is reinforced by the fact that though ice-pitons may be quite secure to move up on, they are frequently not able to arrest a falling leader; so that security on these as on all other ice pitches is chiefly a matter of the leader making absolutely sure of each step, and not on the second's ability to hold him if he does fall, as on rock. It will be seen, then, that though vertical and overhanging walls of ice can be climbed, the overhang will never in practice be very pronounced, nor generally very long. Owing to variations in texture and formation it does not follow that what can be climbed at one time can be so at another. It is emphasised that such pitches are very much the exception, that the technique should be practised on a safe bit of glacier before being tried in a more serious place, and that on any but the fiercest ice climbs the climber who finds himself faced with such a pitch can reckon at once that he is off the route. Reference has already been made to the use of drill and bamboo stakes for the descent, and also to the development of ice-screws. These last should make possible the ascent of much more pronounced overhangs than hitherto, provided the ice is firm, as they can be put in closer to the line of pull.

As with rock-pitons, ice-pitons are often used purely for security. On steep pitches where the party is moving one at a time they are often used as belays, both main and running. A large and comfortable bucket-step is pleasant to have as a stance and aids security but wastes time to cut—and time is another form of security. Each party will work out its own compromise. A capstan can, of course, be cut out of the ice as a belay, but it is quicker to hammer in a peg.   It should be put in as high up as one can reach without stretching, and is best used like an English rock-belay, with the belay taut and the climbing rope held round the waist.   It might be put in at something like a 45 degree angle to the horizontal, a little less when the wall is very steep, a little more if it is very slight: but always at an acute angle to the possible pull.

It may be worth mentioning here, though not strictly in context, another use for the ice-peg.   On slopes between 45 degrees and 65 degrees it will be found that it is possible to crampon without cutting steps with far greater ease and security if the axe is held in one hand and an ice-peg in the other.   Both the peg and the pick of the axe are used like daggers.

Ice pegs are useful to abseil from if there is not time enough to cut a bollard.   Again the peg-pull angle should be acute.   The various pendulum and diagonal methods of rappeling can be applied to ice as well as to rock, but in fact the necessity for them will be extremely rare.   The prusik-loop technique can be adapted to bring seconds up overhangs, and conversely a number of étriers linked together can be very useful in crevasse rescue work.

The mechanics of a full-scale artificial ice pitch are the same as those of one on rock, but the procedure is, perhaps, still more strenuous because of the smaller number of positions the body can adopt, owing to the necessity of not pulling outwards on the pegs. If 12-point crampons are worn it may be possible to dispense with étriers, but it may be preferable to use stirrups of some sort whatever crampons are used so as to keep the strain on the pegs more strictly downward and so as not to tire out the arms. A technique used by some German climbers is to make a seat by suspending an axe on two slings from a peg.   The pegs are usually not put in directly one above the other, but alternately somewhat to the left and right, with one rope in each line.

Once ice-pegs get well and truly frozen in (which takes from two to ten minutes according to the temperature) it is frequently necessary to cut them out, because bashing them around as one would a rock-peg does not always work and may only result in their breaking.

The problems of steep or overhanging snow (as encountered at cornices and bergschrunds) are concentrated in the business of getting something to grip securely. Unless the snow is very hard-frozen, pegs are too small to grip well, and ice-axes have to be used instead. If the snow is hard enough to make it impossible to get these fully in by hand they can be driven in with a peg-hammer. Again it may be easier to use étriers or foot-loops so that the pull comes constantly in the proper direction, but crampons may not have to be worn, depending on the state of the snow. Slings can also be slung on the axes as running belays.

If there is a definite prospect of having to rappel off deep snow the party should carry a stout stake, such as a piece of fence-post sharpened at one end and, perhaps, thirty inches long, which is driven well down into the snow and used as a rappel point. Otherwise an enormous snow - bollard will have to be cut, which is time-wasting, or an ice-axe will have to be sacrificed.

6. Expansion Bolts

The star drill is held against the rock with one hand and struck hard with the hammer. It is twisted slightly between each blow. When the hole thus drilled is judged to be deep enough for use (to save time a rather shallow hole might be used for movement, with a deeper one every fourth or fifth time for security) the bolt is inserted. One type expands automatically as it is hammered in and is then there for good (this is the quickest, lightest and simplest). Another type is slid into the hole, then expanded by tightening with a spanner (the strongest and safest). On to the bolt is now slid the hanger, a small sheet of steel, bent in the middle through about 25 degrees, with

59

a hole in each plane. One hole is slid along the bolt until it is flat against the wall and then secured with a nut. The plane with the other hole is now hanging below the bolt and sticking out slightly from the wall. A karabiner is clipped into this, and the whole contraption then used in exactly the same way as an ordinary piton. If one of the new ring headed bolts is used, no hanger is necessary. The length of time required to insert one bolt may vary from five to twenty minutes according to the hardness of the rock. Owing to this length of time and the strenuosity of such a job in an overhanging position it may be necessary to wear some form of rappel harness which can be clipped on to each bolt in turn as we arrive, and in which one can sit.

GENERAL CONSIDERATIONS

1. Care of Kit

It is a very good thing to oil the gates of karabiners every now and then to prevent them getting rusty or stiff. Nylon ropes and étriers do not rot, but it is a good thing to keep them away from any sources of heat. Hemp ropes, on the other hand, deteriorate easily, and should be dried and stored with the greatest care in a warm airy place. The handles of hammers may be seasoned once a year or so by a simple wipe with linseed oil, but strict care should be taken to keep it away from metal parts as it is apt to start rot where the metal meets the wood. When storing metal things like karabiners or piton hammers it is a good idea to coat them with vaseline. But, perhaps, the most important method of preserving kit is to mark it. Equipment inevitably gets totally mixed up in the process of artificial climbing, and the only way to escape loss is to have a private identification mark stamped or painted on all one's gear, and to sort everything out as soon as a climb is over. It may be worth noting from one point of view or the other that a large number of people use red paint for their mark.

2. Grading

The difficulty of an artificial pitch is judged on its angle, the distance between the pegs and the difficulty of finding places to put them, the security of the pegs, the length of the pitch, and how many of the pegs are already in place.

In the Dolomites any artificial pitch is automatically graded VI. This seems rather unrealistic, as many artificial pitches are equivalent to no more than grade III or IV, and, of course, it fails to discriminate between free and artificial climbing, so that it is difficult to make a prior estimate of a climb. It is odd that such an out of date system should persist in the birthplace and home of "modern" technique.

In the Vallot guide to the range of Mont Blanc a better method has been devised. The pitches of free climbing are still graded from I to VI, but the artificial pitches are graded separately as A1, A2 and A3: the rough equivalence being AI=IV (V. Dif. to mild Severe), A2=V (Severe to mild V.S.), A3=VI (good V.S.). This system has been adopted by English climbers for the artificial climbs that exist in this country.

It is, of course, sometimes very difficult to draw the line between free climbing and artificial. On the continent a pitch would seem to be considered artificial only when it becomes necessary to use tension and étriers. Up till then it is still "free climbing with pegs," which explains the reply to a query about the Fissure Rey which once surprised some English climbers: "no, it is not artificial, you just climb up ze pitons!" Sometimes we come across pitches that contain both free and artificial climbing, and these get a compound grading, such as "A3 and V." It will be found that as in ordinary climbing the actual technical level represented by a given grading is generally higher on outcrops than on mountains, and on certain outcrops the grade A4 has been employed. Though there is still only a comparatively small amount of artificial climbing in this country it will be found that some of it is equal in difficulty to anything that exists abroad.

3. Where to Practise

Though many climbers have picked up their artificial techniques as they have gone along, it is also true that those who have achieved important results have all practised hard on smaller cliffs. It is also not enough to read a book like this one and then think "Oh well! I'll see how it works when I get there." A little practice is worth a lot of theory. A slipshod technique may suffice to get one up a short easy artificial pitch such as the ones on the South ridge of the Fou, the Roc-Grépon traverse, the North ridge of the Peigne or the Chamonix face of the

Aiguille de l'M, but will result in nothing but trouble on the bigger, harder routes of the Mont Blanc range, the Dolomites or elsewhere. To start up the West face of the Dru without considerable artificial experience would be similar to starting up the Khumbu icefall without ever having seen an ice-axe or crampons. The men who have done these big climbs, whether continental or British, have all perfected their technique painstakingly on easier climbs and on outcrops and on smaller hills, such as the Grigna near Lecco, the Salève near Geneva, the Calanques around Marseilles, the Saussois in reach of Paris and Lyon, the Ardennes — or Derbyshire. There are excellent possibilities for practice all over Britain. The granite of the Cornish cliffs is most suitable, but the standard of free climbing is high and pegging should not be abused. Avon Gorge tends to "free climbing with pegs" rather than all-out artificial, but a few pitches exist. A certain amount has been done at Cheddar, but the best possibilities remain. A long line of firm limestone cliffs near Swanage is yielding many excellent routes. In Scotland and Ireland, due to the scale of things, pitons have been employed in a way approximating more to Alpine usage, but there are also practice crags close to Glasgow and Aberdeen. The Northumberland coast also provides scope. A little artificial has been done on the sandstone around Tunbridge Wells but it is not really very suitable, and the same can be said of the chalk-pits and scarps that can be found here and there through the country — yet they are better than nothing, and, faute de mieux, provide an introduction to the basic business of the double rope. The rock in Snowdonia and the Lakes does not lend itself particularly well to peg-climbing, and anyone who tries it there without having first shown that he can master all the free routes will invite ridicule and hard feeling. There is some quite good artificial work on gritstone, the most developed places being Millstone Edge and Lawrencefield at Surprise above Hathersage. The most highly developed cliffs in Britain from this point of view are, however, in the northern limestone areas of the Peak and the Craven Fault. In the Peak one should mention particularly the crags of Stoney Middleton, Matlock High Tor, Miller's Dale, the Manifold Valley and Dovedale. The two classics are perhaps the High Tor Bastion and the White Edge on the Ilam Rock. A guidebook is in the course of preparation. Up in the Craven area of Yorkshire the main crags are Kilnsey, Malham Cove and Gordale Scar. The pegging on these is difficult, steep, and quite often dangerous, but anyone who is at home on it will be at home anywhere, and there is no need to venture too far off the ground until familiarity has been gained through a bit of practice.